The Dig
AND
Hotel Fiesta

THE DIG

and

HOTEL FIESTA

Two volumes of poetry by
Lynn Emanuel

UNIVERSITY OF ILLINOIS PRESS
Urbana and Chicago

This book is printed on acid-free paper.

The Dig, a 1991 selection of the National Poetry Series, was first
published in 1992 by the University of Illinois Press.

Hotel Fiesta, first published in 1984 by the University of Georgia
Press, was supported by a grant from the National Endowment for
the Arts, a federal agency.

Library of Congress Cataloging-in-Publication Data

Emanuel, Lynn, 1949–
    The dig and hotel fiesta : two volumes of poetry / by Lynn
Emanuel.
        p.   cm.
    ISBN 0-252-06420-8 (paper)
    I. Title
PS3555.M34A6   1995
811'.54—dc20   94-7703
                                                  CIP

Jeffrey, Jeffrey, Jeffrey, Jeffrey, Jeffrey

Contents

Hotel Fiesta

Prologue:
The Politics of Narrative—Why I Am a Poet

Jill's a good kid who's had some tough luck. But that's another story. It's Friday, and the smell of fish from Tib's hash house is so strong you could build a garage on it. We are sitting in the Blue Lite where Carl has just built us a couple of solid highballs. He's okay, Carl is, if you don't count his Roamin' hands and Rushin' fingers. Then again, that should be the only trouble we have in this life. Anyway, Jill says, "Why don't you tell about it? Nobody every gets the broad's point of view." I don't know, maybe she's right. Jill's just a kid, but she's been around; she knows what's what.

So, I tell Jill, we're at the Blue Lite just like now when he comes in. And the first thing I notice is his hair, which has been Vitalis-ed into submission. But honey, it won't work, and it gives him a kind of rumpled, your-boudoir-or-mine look. I don't know why I noticed that before I noticed his face. Maybe it was the highballs doing the looking. Anyway, then I see his face, and I'm telling you—I'm telling Jill—this is a masterpiece of a face.

But—and this is the god's own truth—I'm tired of beauty. Really, I know, given all that happened, this must sound kind of funny, but it made me tired just to look at him. That's how beautiful he was, and how much he spelled T-R-O-U-B-L-E. So I threw him back. I mean, I didn't *say* it, I say to Jill, with my mouth. But I said it with my eyes and my shoulders. I said it with my heart. I said, Honey, I'm throwing you back. And looking back, that was the worst, I mean the worst thing—bar none—that I could have done, because it drew him like horseshit draws flies. I mean, he didn't walk over and say, "Hello, girls. Hey, you with the dark hair, your indifference draws me like horseshit draws flies."

But he said it with his eyes. And then he smiled. And that smile was a gas station on a dark night. And as wearing as all the rest of it. I'm many things, but dumb isn't one of them. And here is where I say to Jill, "I just can't go on." I mean, how we get from the smile into the bedroom, how it all happens, and what all happens, just bores me. I'm kind of a conceptual storyteller. In fact, I'm kind of a conceptual liver.

I prefer the cookbook to the actual meal. Feeling bores me. That's why I write poetry. In poetry you just give the instructions to the reader and say, "Reader, you go on from here." And what I like about poetry is its readers, because those are giving people. I mean, those are people you can trust to get the job done. They pull their own weight. If I had to have someone at my back in a dark alley, I'd want it to be a poetry reader. They're not like some people who maybe do it right if you tell them, "Put this foot down, and now put that one in front of the other, button your coat, wipe your nose."

So, really, I do it for the readers who work hard and, I feel, deserve something better than they're used to getting. I do it for the working stiffs. And I write for people like me who are just tired of the trickle-down theory where some guy spends ages and pages on some fat book where everything, including the draperies, which happen to be *burnt orange,* is described, and, further, is some *metaphor* for something. And this whole boggy waste trickles down to the reader in the form of a little burp of feeling. God, I hate prose. I think the average reader likes ideas.

"A sentence, unlike a line, is not a station of the cross." I said this to the poet Mark Strand. I said, "I could not stand to write prose. I could not stand to have to write things like 'the draperies were burnt orange and the carpet was brown.'" And he said, "You could do it if that's all you did, if that was the beginning and the end of your novel." So, please, don't ask me for a little trail of bread crumbs to get from the smile to the bedroom and from the bedroom to the death at the end, although you can ask me a lot about death. That's all I like, the very beginning and the very end. I haven't got the stomach for the rest of it.

I don't think many people do. But, like me, they're either too afraid or too polite to say so. That's why the movies are such a disaster. Now *there's* a form of popular culture that doesn't have a clue. Movies should be five minutes long. You should go in, see a couple of shots, maybe a room with orange draperies and a rug. A voice-over would say, "I'm having a hard time getting Raoul, the protagonist, from the hotel room into the elevator." And bang, that's the end. The lights come on; everybody walks out full of sympathy because this is a shared experience. Everybody in that theater knows how hard it is to get Raoul from the hotel room into the elevator. Everyone has had to do boring, dogged work. Everyone has lived a life that seems to inflict upon every vivid moment the smears, fingerings, and pawings of plot and feeling. Everyone has lived under this oppression. In other words, everyone has had to eat shit—day after day, the endless meals they didn't want, those dark, half-gelatinous lakes of gravy that lay on the plate like an ugly rug, and that wrinkled clump of reddish-orange roast beef that looks like it was dropped onto your plate from a great height. God what a horror: getting Raoul into the elevator.

And that's why I write poetry. Honey, in poetry, you don't do that kind of work.

THE DIG

THE BEGINNING

(Ely, Nevada)

I have decided on a place to eat in at midday, a
place to eat in at night, a place to have my drink
in after dinner. I have arranged my little life.
—Jean Rhys

Stone Soup

She wants to get born, so she invents a mother
to hold the long wooden wand of a cooking
spoon fast in her fist, the big black zero
of the iron pot, the stone of the pig's knuckle,
the buzz of the fridge, the tap scalding the soap
into suds, the tureen dunked, again, again;
she invents the tintinnabulation of the milkman's
bottles in their wire basket and the sigh
of the clutch as he disappears and the match
that touches the gas burner—the blue root,
the little tiara of yellow fire. Beyond the window
it is nearly dark, a sudsy ocean is coughing up
a beach as gray and hard as poured concrete.
She has set herself a task, like a train lugging
its hard body toward Portland, so she now makes
a father's coat come home from the day shift,
its pockets drooping like the jowls of a hound,
and his long black shoes with their dew of glitter
under the fluorescent light of the breakfast nook,
his mustache like a school janitor's brooms;
she begins with talk of labor and wages,
his big hand turning over the leaves of the light
and water bills like a boring book;
it will not be long now until she will make them
make her from nothing, a stone, a pot.

The Planet Krypton

Outside the window the McGill smelter
sent a red dust down on the smoking yards of copper,
on the railroad tracks' frayed ends disappearing
into the congestion of the afternoon. Ely lay dull

and scuffed: a miner's boot toe worn away and dim,
while my mother knelt before the Philco to coax
the detonation from the static. From the Las Vegas
Tonapah Artillery and Gunnery Range the sound

of the atom bomb came biting like a swarm
of bees. We sat in the hot Nevada dark, delighted,
when the switch was tripped and the bomb hoisted
up its silky, hooded, glittering, uncoiling length;

it hissed and spit, it sizzled like a poker in a toddy.
The bomb was no mind and all body; it sent a fire
of static down the spine. In the dark it glowed like the coils
of an electric stove. It stripped every leaf from every

branch until a willow by a creek was a bouquet
of switches resinous, naked, flexible, and fine.
Bathed in the light of KDWN, Las Vegas,
my crouched mother looked radioactive, swampy,

glaucous, like something from the Planet Krypton.
In the suave, brilliant wattage of the bomb, we were
not poor. In the atom's fizz and pop we heard possibility
uncorked. Taffeta wraps whispered on davenports.

A new planet bloomed above us; in its light
the stumps of cut pine gleamed like dinner plates.
The world was beginning all over again, fresh and hot;
we could have anything we wanted.

Chinoisserie

My mother in her dress of red Viyella, teetering like a tiny idol
on three-inch lacquered spikes, chignon dressed with little gold-
throated bells that chirped more sweetly than the cricket,
held her small, perfect hands to the torrent pouring from the slots.
Money went like water through our fingers: was dammed
by budgets, released, then abruptly gone at the China Starr,
that grotto, festooned with red and vivid lanterns.
Dark as the inside of a limousine, that saloon was where
our lives, dulled by the copper barons, were cleansed,
where we bade good-bye to the limp and stutter
of bad goods, to the wince of the creaky rocker, to the vast
grandmother dying in its clutch, to the dirty, wrinkled ones
and tens pieced together to cover the week. Hello, we said,
to the beautiful dark starlit bar and the luxury therein:
the runcible spoons with their slippery cargo: the snarled silk
of tinned bean sprout, the wrinkled flame of the dried lily.
Hunched over our beakers of jasmine tea, we let the exotic
rinse over us—impractical and non-negotiable.

Blonde Bombshell

Love is boring and passé, all the old baggage,
the bloody bric-a-brac, the bad, the gothic,
retrograde, obscurantist hum and drum of it
needs to be swept away. So, night after night,
we sit in the dark of the Roxy beside grandmothers
with their shanks tied up in the tourniquets
of rolled stockings and open ourselves, like earth
to rain, to the blue fire of the movie screen
where love surrenders suddenly to gangsters
and their cuties. There in the narrow,
mote-filled finger of light, is a blonde
so blonde, so blinding, she is a blizzard, a huge
spook, and lights up like the sun the audience
in its galoshes. She bulges like a deuce coupe.
When we see her we say good-bye to Kansas.
She is everything spare, cool, and clean,
like a gas station on a dark night or the cold
dependable light of rage coming in on schedule like a bus.

One Summer Hurricane Lynn Spawns Tornados as Far West as Ely

The storm with my name dragged one
heavy foot over the roads of the county.
It was a bulge in a black raincoat, pointed
and hard as the spike in a railroad tie;
it dipped like a dowser's rod and screamed
like the express at the bend at Elko.
It made the night feverish and the sky
burn with the cold blue fire of a motel sign.
Oh that small hell of mine nipped at the town,
turned the roads to mud, lingered at the horizon,
a long clog, a sump. All sigh and lamentation,
the whole city of grief rose up to face that black
boot that waited to kick us open like a clay pot.

The Night Man at the Blue Light

Luther Benton is talking to his heart again.
She can see it through the smeared window
of the Blue Lite Motel & Lounge, his mouth
ajar at bored Rita, the waitress, lifting
a cigarette to the scarlet crescent of her smile.
He is talking to his heart while the grillman
loses himself in the news and in one corner
of Ely the juke delivers the goods. I love him
in love—my grandfather's hired man. Bringing
in the morning coffee, he would say with a whistle
Be still my heart and then succumb to one
or another bad line of credit that came in
to work on a drunk under the liquid stare
of a ten-point buck. Night after night
he'd peer at the darkened windows, the smear
of moon, listening to the lovers groaning
over the oiled switches of his remembrance
until above the Snake Range a dawn
of unrequited love rose like the Kingdom of Heaven.
No one for miles. No one
in those golden streets, but Luther.

Outside Room Six

Down on my knees again, on the linoleum outside room six,
I polish it with the remnant of Grandpa's union suit,
and once again dead Grandma Fry looks down on me
from Paradise and tells me from the balcony of wrath
I am girlhood's one bad line of credit.

Every older girl I know is learning how to in a car,
while here I am, eye at the keyhole, watching Raoul,
who heats my dreams with his red hair, lights up my life
with his polished brogues, groans *Jesus, Jesus.*
I am little and stare into the dark until the whole small

town of lust emerges. I stare with envy, I stare and stare.
Now they are having cocktails. The drinks are dim lagoons
beneath their paper parasols. The air is stung with orange,
with lemon, a dash of Clorox, a dash of bitters;
black square, white square goes the linoleum.

Dreaming of Rio at Sixteen

It was always Raoul's kisses or grandmother's
diamond earrings that burned like Brazilian noons
while you and she sheeted beds finding every
beautiful mother an excuse to stop and look
as they moved in sling-back shoes past Lloyd's
Esso then into the movies' cool arcades.

Taking off your clothes, sometimes sixteen was
that, sometimes it was not naked but wore
a collar at its throat and gloves, kissed
with its mouth closed, over and over, like the pinch
of a tight shoe. Even all buttoned up, sixteen
was semitropic and summer had put out every lure:

a whole plantation of perfect grasses.
Lynnskala, Lynnksala your grandmother called,
her voice grinding uphill, heavier and heavier,
with its load of anger. Old stab in the dark
stood on the back porch stirring her spoon around
in the dinner bell and calling you in the voice that now

held its hands across its heart, *Come home, come
home, save yourself for a wedding,* while you,
beside the Amazon, were all teeth, all boat.

For Me at Sunday Sermons, the Serpent

coming lightly, perfectly
 into the garden
  was as smart as Eve was

pink, fat & pliant,
 was tough as a root,
  but blue

or green:
 a reed, a stem;
  the uninterruptedness of him

from tail to lip, all
 one thing, consistent
  as a walking stick.

Or he was a ruby
 cummerbund, a glove
  on its way to the opera

dropped
 in the dust
  of this godforsaken town.

Beside his motionless chill,
 Ely, Nevada,
  was as dull as two buttons.

He was the green
 light, the go-ahead,
  the spark, the road,

the ticket out.

BEGINNING AGAIN

Poverty is your treasure. Do not exchange it
for an easy life.

—Zen-Getsu

This Is the Truth

Now, this is the truth of that particular fiction,
sweet angel, I mean, she hopes you do not buy
all that sweet domesticity, that tenderness and yielding.
She remembers her father only vaguely,
the glittering wreckage of his black hair,
rinsed in oils, the sap of melting pomade
that leaked from his sideburns which he dabbed
with a hankie. He inhabited his armchair
like a black cloud. Glum. Cultivated.
His temper was a downed power line
that fishtailed back and forth across their lives.
Lethal Hits. Near Misses. To avoid it
they crept for miles over dangerous passes
to Ely, my precious, they had stolen a car,
and were on the run, sleeping in tacky motel
rooms, cooking on a hot plate,
terrified and poor at last, oh my darling girl,
as you can only be when you have become
a fugitive from the domestic life and are blessed
with nothing that anyone could want,
free and out of luck and poor, poor at last.

Domestic Violence

The night is dark as mother's closet with its big woolens.
In the kitchen a piece of pork hisses in a black pan,
oiled in its own fat, pink and wrinkled as a baby's ass.
Not how can it be imagined, but how not, how not
to be there, under the ceiling bulb where shadows
swell, slacken—sails in the winds of an argument—
of a man with the whole dim tribe of womanhood.
To the left, the parlor, the bulges and ruptures
of broken springs and stuffing, the davenport's
red velvet like the blush of blood that comes
through the crushed ice on the cooler's dead pike.
Along the split rail fence, the white hens bloom
in a line, pale, squat little ghosts, and the far door
of the Pentecostal church is all light and holler;
the uncontrollable pleasure of blessedness dies
to the low shiver of the hymns, then the reverend's
fist pounds the air as though to make someone
who is getting up stumble and fall down again.

What the Keyhole Was

A bare room, an empty bucket,
a curtain tied back with string,
the moon a yellow paring cut
from grandma's heel when she sat
glued to the pure, cold, blue cube
of light that was the television,
that glacial presence that cooled
and soothed. It was that little world
within a world which, being god,
you could shut and open up.
Closeted without supper, you wore
the big black hollows of mother's
patent leathers back and forth,
to the keyhole of the guest room.
Begin with the technical problems
of lust, with a woman all down,
with a man all up. Begin with this
or that that coaxed the hand to touch
it, the zippers, the cuffs, the sighs
lopped off by kisses, the body
before your eyes becomes a river of sighs
and you standing there,
both Diana and Actaeon,
Agamemnon and Helen,
Sodom and the wife of Lot.

Seizure

This was the winter mother told time by my heart
ticking like a frayed fan belt in my chest.
This was the fifties & we were living on nothing
& what of her, the black girl, my own black nurse,
what of her who arrived on Greyhound in the heart
of so dramatic a storm it froze the sleeves at her wrists
& each nostril was rimed with white like salt on a glass,
what of her who came up the dark stair on the limp of her
own bad ticker, weary, arrogant, thin, her suitcase noosed
with rope, in the grip of a rage she came, a black woman,
into our white lives, like a splinter, & stayed. Charming
& brilliantly condescending, she leaned down to kiss "the baby,"
& hissed *my little princess* & hushed the Jordan & set the chariots
on the golden streets & *Mother*, I cried to her, & went out like a light.

Whites

The scar, the moon, the blind man's cane, the gluey soup of barley,
the bread, the milk, the chalked concoctions that coat the ulcer,
the blind man's eye, the banker's long, pale, trembling fingers
poking at the family ledgers until even the neighbors come by
to get a look at folks so relentlessly unsuccessful. The tubers,

the roots, long and damp and weeping, the nurses' noses stuck
into our business. Weevils in sacks of spoiled flour,
grandmother's feet pared with a paring knife, Dulles, Eisenhower.
Glaciers' paunches, slow and heavy, the body of the Savior
on the altar wall, in the tub upstairs, Pierre, the naked sailor.

Drawing Rosie's Train Trip

I begin with the tree's left foot,
the long, black, raw, wet root

stubbing a toe in the dirt.
I begin with the cloud on its back,

the train at the horizon small & black
as a swarm of gnats,

with my right thumb
dumb as a puppy & squat & fat

as an old woman stooping over
the mess I have made of her garden;

& now the train is gnawing
its way through the meadow, going

like Columbus toward the end of the world.
The garden has dried to a dish of mud.

The tree's shadow is coming toward me
stiffly & slowly as an old woman's leg

in a black stocking
& now the clouds come carrying

their own white hankies, waving
good-bye & one bad child is squalling.

The Idol

In the kitchen a black blur
turns its blind face to stare.
I let it look. I am nothing,

seven, among the props of bankruptcy
(the pen, and banker, and pale ledger)
where grandmother is turning to stone

under two slow oars of the ceiling fan.
Big as a houseboat in her slip,
she sits in the fiery block of red

upholstery that is a leather armchair
and watches the capitals of Europe fall
again, in the fires of the TV screen

while trucks boil down Route 6
to where the atom bomb is parked,
out in the desert near Tonapah.

When they dig that geyser out
of the ground it does not bend
or nod, but clings to the horizon

pale, intent, shy, and proud.
At night it smolders in the slot
between two silos while Ely

burns like a lit fuse between two
beautiful small black hills.
Looking up from the fire in the hold

of the big black iron warship of the stove,
a groan rises in the flue of grandma's throat
like smoke off a lamp wick

and her heart, down on one knee,
puts down the other.

What Grieving Was

That was not the summer of aspic
and cold veal. It was so hot

the car seat stung my thighs
and the rearview mirror swam

with mirage. In the back seat
the leather grip was noosed by twine.

We were not poor but we had
the troubles of the poor.

She who had been that soft snore
beside the Nytol, open-mouthed,

was gone, somewhere, somewhere
there was a bay, there was a boat,

there was a scold in mother's mouth.
What I remember best

is the way everything came and went
in the window of my brief attention.

At the wake I was beguiled
by the chromium yellow lemon pies.

The grandfather clock's pendant
of unaffordable gold told the quarter hour.

The hearse rolled forward over the O's
of its own surprise.

What Ely Was

The mauve, the ocher of canned tamales, the dark silt
of gravy burning, the hominy's white knuckles;
fats that made a surface gleam like a pigeon's neck,
like a spill of gasoline, melt-down crusts of oleo
on the tuna casserole, toast that was blackened
to a piece of macadam, a singed field, a roof shingle.
The cool unguent of jam upon a spoon, but every sweet
thing has a sting. It was good for you, this needle, this pin.
Under the beautiful blue glass dome of plum preserves
was the bite of penicillin. I longed for chocolate both
sweet and bitter, fried green plantain, mustard, onion,
red tomato, rice and black beans in a pot, Moroccan olives
with cayenne, Haut-Brion, cabbage, ham. Somewhere
some green coast exported all I wanted of all I wanted,
a kingdom where my hunger fit, both mind and body, all of it.

A Red Kimono

I stare at the brass scarred by beating until
it is as bright and uneven as a lake in August when the sun
melts all reflections into one wide gold zero, when the sky
itself is wide, is hot as the bell that this schoolmaster,
insupportably strict, tips to summon the children from the unrelenting
heat of noon. The long tape unrolls from the teeth of the adding
machine onto the scarred deal. Over and over the budget unreels
and spills, liberated from the sprockets and machinery of will.
My mother sits with a pencil and ticks her teeth, we are broke,
every avenue of escape is closed, even the car tires at the curb
are fat black zeros, all the scheming and coaxing, the wringing
of every cent from every dollar, has come to nothing. I watch
my mother swab up the dust, her hair tied in a rag, her naked
feet, nails bloodied by a tiny brush. Misery, misery, the cranes
of good luck hunch at the snowy mountain of her left breast
as she bends to set the empties on the step in the housecoat
the landlady lent.

Past and Present

Many a woman has a past; but I am told she has at least a dozen, and that they all fit.
                                                    —Oscar Wilde

The Past

Where did she come from, that dig
in the ribs? Who is she to pretend
she's me and to take on that ditched-in,
hopeless tone? Who is this phony
yokel? This two-dollar bill, this
pig knuckle? Honey, I tell her,
my name is Lynn Collins Emanuel,
someone whose whole manner says
I'm over-educated but recovering,
I have been to Europe and I don't
even recall that stain in the road
that you refer to as Ely, Nevada;
oh please, I think, give me a break,
woman, I mean who would believe
this arms-akimbo-in-faded-calico
West Coast depiction of the West?
Get out of here with your fibs
and lesions, your deaf ear wired
to its hearing aid, your coughs
and wattles. I know stories about
Gertrude Stein in her silk socks
drunk on Bordeaux in the garden.
What do I want to sit at your table for,
to be passed the faded confetti
of the succotash, the turkey
trussed like a hostage? Listen,
I am money in the bank, swank,
with it, well informed, full
of a Semitic glamour, doleful,
sleek and dark, shit, honey,
how did you get by the bouncer,
editor-within-me, Mr. Right?

And why am I now, like a new tenant,
moving into the little varicosity
on your left calf, the nylons knotted
just above the knee and, further,
into the hands that held that soft
gray lump of rag and washed,
and washed again the greasy
Formica of the dinner table?
How did I get to be at the head
of a long line of unlucky
women with their propensity
for poverty, influenza,
weak chests, and bad judgment,
how did their troubles get to be mine?
And no, I don't know who
could be in that hand-dug grave
at the Rosebud Cemetery, the little
dusty picket fence of teeth smiling up
from that too-shallow niche is
not mine. I don't know who
she is. I've never seen her.
I was in Paris at the time.

Bella Roma

Into the distances of the afternoon
the barges carrying blood oranges from Spain
crawl across the Tiber's wrinkled length,
the sun like a communion wafer stained
with wine dips down, the moon rises
through these windows. Giacommeto
is in love with me, I am having a crisis
of the spirit. Oh Roma, both garden
and lazaretto, in your dark streets
the sailors still swagger home
to brothels late at night, drunk,
vicious, potent.
I see the gray olive trees cloud
the skies, but their jewels, bright,
green, hard wink at me *emerald, emerald.*
I am ashamed to be so poor, so full
of lust with laddered stockings
and soiled cuffs, with buttons drooping
from their threads; I am ashamed to grow old,
each eye with its delta of wrinkles, so that anyone who
passes
reads you like a map of where you've been,
the line beside the mouth is the street to the Black
Cat Café, the whole face like an unmade bed.
Will I have enough for rent? Enough to clean the black dress?

Riddle

Like the queens and prostitutes at the French court:
all outwardness, all silks and corsets,
the wind among them, my mother's voice.
Inside, the waitress in a dull apron,
the flat pan of her face chipped and pitted;

first, I noticed how conventionally plain
she was, then the gold-stubbled lip
over which a lover's tongue could wander.
All one summer my hunger lunged for this
or that green calabash whose name was as hollow

as the sound of wooden tackle blown knocking
at a mast, or as round as the throat of a well
down which I tossed my wishes to hear them throb
a message: *artichoke, artichoke.*

Who Is She Kidding

Who is she kidding? Who is she,
anyway, talking as though she knew
when, I can tell you, honey, she never
even saw an artichoke until she was
eighteen and went to Italy and got laid
for the first time on the beach outside
Talamone, and even then
that girl didn't know how to spell
artichoke until she was twenty-three.
But honey, you can't fit a girl like that
into the straitjacket of a book of poems.
I mean no book of poems in the world
is big enough to explain how she got
from Ely, Nevada, to Talamone getting
laid, so she just moves along as though
poetry were an interstate and here we are
passing Ely, here we are copulating
with Marco, all the little stitches
of explaining have been cut.
We may faint dead away before she's
going to tell us what the truth is,
but honey, I'll tell you one thing, life's
like its cooking and Ely was spinach
untinned by Grandma directly onto
the plate so that its brackish
backwash broke into waves and,
leaking, weeping, flooded the hominy.
It dripped off the china the way
Columbus thought the sea dripped
off the lip at the end of the world.
Whole ships rode off into its darkness,
the coffers of nations were squandered.

*Artichoke, my god, this one could sell
snow to the Eskimos; this is America,
honey, we don't need any damned artichokes.*

Self-Portrait at Eighteen

Today I became my own secret admirer, unearthing
from the junk—the boxes of napkins tatted by Grandmother
and Great Aunt Tiny, the cobwebby bulk of table linens
that covered the scab of scratched deal that was their kitchen
table where they gave thanks and passed the faded confetti
of the succotash—this photograph. It is not a flash of family
dinner, but a luminous window, the faded wash of clouds
strung up in Talamone. Somewhere at the rim a somewhat darker,
rumpled mass of—what?—the photographer's jacket, or the blanket
where, after buying two tabs of acid from a boy who sold
a handful along the shore, we made love and then set out to
sabotage respectability or, at least in my case, self-regard.
In the foreground a fringe of reeds suggests the landscape
blinked at this girl-stretched-naked-on-the-sand,
although *stretched* implies passivity, loss of will, and clearly
this is a willful, though awkward, abandonment, an act
of exposure not merely meant but mutinous. Uncanny
the resemblance of the pose—awkward, although not innocent—
to an inexperienced lounge singer, maybe a girl leaning
uneasily against a black piano; she has knuckled under
to convention but clearly not enough or generously.
Still, I love the delicate bones of my pelvis (the bony repose
that suggests, as well, the sculptures on sarcophagi)
in this photograph which a not-quite-forgotten-enough
photographer entitled: *Portrait of a Woman, Nude.*

We, the Poets of America,

don't have time for Istanbul,
the Cave of the Ropemaker.
We are like you, America,
when you were a rough draft,
a marsh, a swamp, newt and savannah.

Like those nebulae of dust
that wave and shiver in the black
window of the universe,
we are lost hankies waiting
to belong to somebody,

unclaimed and unloved.
We're old coins plucked
too late from the acid,
blurred and softened faces
you can turn over in your hands,

toys and thimbles that grief
got squeezed into, all your sins
come home to roost.
Here we stand on your dark dock
beside the warty parcel of our

baggage, lifting a hand to watch
the sun's red wheel turn the gulf
to blood, watching the sun disappear
like a gold doubloon into the black
knuckles of the Adirondacks.

Lame foot by lame foot, we come
tapping at your sagging screens

in soiled gloves, matrons of sorrow
and mistake, runs of bad luck
trying to make the connection

between you and the small potatoes.
And that is not the worst.
We have come to point out all
your mistakes chalked blurrily
on the beyond's blurry slates,

to tell you that you're a blot and hell
is vacant, dirty, dark and that there's
nothing for miles but tragedy and grief
and a squad of girls like us with which
to spend eternity, dusting the infernal dust.

Inspiration

I am tired of the tundra of the mind,
where a few shabby thoughts hunker
around a shabby fire. All day from my window
I watch girls and boys hanging out
in the dark arcades of adolescent desire.

Tonight, everything is strict with cold,
the houses closed, the ice botched by skaters.
I am tired of saying things about the world,
and yet, sometimes, these streets are so
slick and bold they remind me of the wet

zinc bar at the Café Marseilles, and suddenly the sea
is green and lust is everywhere in a red cravat,
leaning on his walking stick and whispering,
I am a city, you are my pilgrim,
meet me this evening. Love, Pierre.

And so I have to get up and walk downstairs
just to make sure the city's still secure
in its leafless and wintery slime
and it still is and yet somewhere on that
limitless, starlit seacoast of my past,

Pierre's red tie burns like a small fire.
And all at once my heart stumbles like a
drunken sailor, and I am adrift in the *bel aujourd'hui* of Ely.

Heartsick

I had enough bad luck that summer,
I had enough bad weather, too, the sun
lacquered the windows across the street
that were shut against the heat of noon;
staring out at them from behind the dim
screen of the terminal I knew my neighbors
were sweating in their dark bedrooms,
foreheads leaked on by cooling compresses.

I was spending the summer getting diagnosed,
trudging the hot and littered streets for weekly
visits to a doctor so expensive and remote
my voice shook when I called for my
appointment, and even now he seems
to me a tall white blur in a white coat.
I was not myself. In that heat
my heart had reestablished its old
bad habit of skipping a beat so that
suddenly I felt like a factory out of work,
all the machinery went still, the silence
was deafening and quick, dying seemed
within, then out of reach.

I throve on this medical melodrama, my ill health
sustained me over the bad places until
the police called at seven A.M. to tell me
Raoul Flores had been picked up for vagrancy
on a traffic island in Lake Street and, not awake,
I said, I'm sorry I don't know any Raoul.

Then there was a blank place, the sound of a precinct,
not sound, really, but to sound what a Xerox

is to print and then a voice—his—but so condensed,
tiny, light, like an insect, like the ghost of a ghost,
Lynn, I need a place to spend the night, it said.

I was not impressed. I did not want to be
disturbed by reveries or guilt, but, all right,
yes, I said, take a taxi, I'll pay
when you get here. And I did.
Because when the door of the taxi
opened and he ducked out into the sun,
sorrow and love kicked me so hard
in the chest my heart just stopped;
it seemed to say, I cannot bear it, you
go on without me. And I did, I walked
down the walk and stood while he
handed my money to the driver
and everything began to take on preternatural

detail. I noticed the shoulder of his leather jacket
scratched and scuffed, and my heart rose up
out of its stutter, its limp, when the next beat
seemed to drip from it achingly, infinitely
slowly, and never arrive, and that dark barn
behind the Blue Lite opened its doors to me
again and I let myself be backed against
the dirty bale, warm against my butt, as this boy,
part gall, part oil, ran his hand below my boned bra
and whispered, *Is this the Maginot Line?*
while I grew just idiotic with anxiety and lust.

On Waking after Dreaming of Raoul

If Freud was right and dreams of falling are
dreams of having fallen then you must have been
the beautiful declivity of that hill, Raoul,
the speed was so seductive and the brakes so
unreliable, and so intricate and so abstract
that when I touched them they squeaked like a jar lid
coming loose and I was embarrassed, but not sad,
at being the one flat wheel that bumped down the hill
in an unsteady gulp of denial—oh no oh no oh no—
until I woke up chilly, damp, my breath unsteady.

In order to recover I sit at the desk studying the Order
of the Holy Ghost Retreat and Old Age Home
until dusk comes down the street elm by elm, here
where they've managed to cure them with a tincture
so poisonous the leaves, though living, are frail
and blanched. I think of you, Ruby Flores's
half-brother and a thief and a cook.
Because what good is it anymore, pretending
I didn't love you; after all these years you must
be jailed or dead, and it is a relief to give up
reticence which as you once said is merely
impetuosity held tightly in check.

Over the gold swells of sunset lawns the old
men come rolling in their iron chairs, pushed
around by nuns, their open mouths are O's
of permanent dismay. Far away the stars are
a fine talcum dusting my mother's one good black
dress, those nights she gunned the DeSoto
around Aunt Ada's bed of asters while you shortened
the laces of my breath. Despite the nuns, despite

45

my mother and my own notions of how bad girls
end up educated and alone, the door opens and you

walk in, naked, you, narrow and white
as the fishing knife's pearl handle, and you kiss me
until my resolve grows as empty as the dress
from which I step, both brave and willful.
I loved you, although I didn't know it yet,
anymore than these old men on the dole
of some nun's affectionate disdain
knew that they would end up poor,
mortgaged to a ghost, and living in a place like this.

The Technology of Love

I loved the women of Ely, Nevada, who drank, wept,
and waited out their pasts among the lint
and pins of Roman Catholic self-denial.
Tonight I have come home to watch the girls
of those girls climb the steps of Saint Agnes
while I sit studying the forest of their lit candles
in the open door until the Erie comes past,
black as a seizure, right on schedule.
As a child I sweated out the evening watching
the windows burn in the house of prostitution
that opened when the whole town slept—
even the tiers of saucers at the Beaufort Cafeteria,
even the blues in Ruby's black Victrola.
No matter what I remember I remember that
when she walked down the street all the men
grew still as flags on a still day; I remember
my Great Aunt Ada telling her I told you so
about the sailor whose shadow did a rumba
on Ruby's wall and left her in a flat blaze
of remorse where she drifted for years
visiting every island in the long archipelago of lust.
I loved helping her home, dead drunk,
through the streets of Ely; this world
is no earthly paradiso she told my grandfather
who being my grandfather was looking at the madam
in her black capris, or studying the technology of love:
pawnshop windows filled with wedding rings and guns,
that summer when, glum and drunk, Ruby drove
her blue Impala into the cottonwood on Lagunitas Boulevard.
The only thing that bored Ruby more than God was poetry,
so tonight I have come home to write something plain
as a woman in her grave and watch the girls come out of church

counting up their sins and graces, safe in this last outpost
of the conventional unlike Ruby who is a remembrance and dread
that go beyond what I can bear remembering and further, so deep
she sweeps away all doctrines and boast, that woman teasing
her lures against the current, that ark in its loose gown of oared water.

Rebirth

Today, Braddock Avenue's a parade
moving hood to bumper into the gloom.
The cold front is here from Canada.
All the maples shoulder the snow but
still the storm comes down gothic
and furious and still the long horns
of angry autos sound. Bolder and bolder
that boy from across the street becomes
everything the storm's chill purity
isn't. He's coming my way, again,
leaning toughly on the bell, to sell
me chances for a trip to Acapulco
and suddenly I am in love with his
wayward interest in my living room.

I believe you should go for it
he says and, yes, the stuck door
of imagination opens to the pure
blue gameboard of a swimming pool,
streets cooled by the wash water
and brooms of Hispanic women who are
so beautiful they loosen the long
laces of his breath. And I, full
of divorce and bluster, am coming
up from a beach wearing the slick
cool silver of my naked self and
composing two stanzas of such luminous
uncertainty they make eternity's
stopped clock run and hope is poking
her nose into everything
and I am speechless with rebirth.

A Poem Like an Automobile Can Take You Anywhere,

but you have to wait until Mother gets loaded
on the Greyhound and the bus blotted up
by the black of tobacco at the end of Rook Street
in Bannock, Georgia; until someone's
Aunt Rita, up to her neck again in hot water,
dries the last damp dimple and sweeps away
the constellation of Dier Kiss spilled on her

dressing table, before the plot can come lunging,
purring up to the door of the rental cottage.
It says, We'll go for a spin, and you say, D'accord!
thinking of Paris where a vague and soigné sun
rises forever above the seriously drunk, thinking
of Greece where you can fall in love with the sailors.

And suddenly the room's perfumed with lust
the sheet's a slick and dangerous road
where coupes of French hoods fishtail
like downed power lines and lurch and zoom
and billboards—Giant! White! Immaculate!—
are flying past and the boglands are in bloom.

And now your curiosity begins to travel
like a caravan, each pack animal loaded
with its weight of questions. Why has
the Gare de Lyon bulging at the horizon
huge, manly, tough, turned out to be
a grandpa in his waders among the sycamores?

There in the dark oblong of the windshield
a field of wheat comes swarming toward you
and hicks with open arms welcome you

to Ely, its parlors filled with the little iambs
of Granny's rocker, its sky damp and gray and chilly.

Lost in this wilderness, American and corny,
you stare at the trees and compose new
stanzas of such extravagant uncertainty that,
like "Uncle Raoul" whom you watched on
your knees through the keyhole, who lit up
your life with his burnished lassoes, they groan,
Jesus, Jesus, enough, enough.

THE HEREAFTER AND AFTER THAT

As we went out and in
Between Her final Room
And Rooms where Those to be alive
Tomorrow were, a Blame

That Others could exist
While She must finish quite
A Jealousy for Her arose
so nearly infinite—
                    —Emily Dickinson

Far

I will study her longing for far, for everything
to be more

must travel by eye and she (that more distant
I) will set no limits.

Let the far be everything
subsumed by it. She cannot see the far,

she must be it.
Oh far, oh far, she sighs,

to be what you are—all air and view—
not this stubborn body, this root

clutching at its curb of dirt,
but to live behind the eyes, at the eave

and attic of myself, halloo, halloo.
And yet, oddly, they hold each other

near and far, she and I, a landscape—
this house and these two willows,

cowlicky, disheveled, humped up
against the windows

admitting the little wrists and fingers
of the sparrows.

This is how the trees solve far,
they do not watch it like a house

as she does now, here
she is, that glittering window, that eye

beyond the churchyard and the green
smudge which is the osiers.

Oh my own far self, I know you are there,
leanly watchful and at ease.

The far is alert, like you, like me.
When the bell's lead throats are filled with clappers

that attainable sweet beyond
is drowned by their wild we are, we are.

Inspiration, Two

Birds in the morning are a moving blur
several blurs in the windows.

And this moon—
aloof, amused, complacent, idle, unitary—

is feeling sorry for itself
watching me through the window

of another description of itself.
The moon, like any of us,

analytic and introspective,
wants to have light shed on its light.

But it's snowing.
Not a sight in the world can stop it.

I let my sulk wash over me
and it grows dark enough and sad.

The problem is how to say
smartly what is used to being said beautifully, only.

A black cave.
My thoughts and I have parted ways.

I settle into a primitive loaf
when suddenly into that dark comes

a gazelle with horns as fine as two steel bits.
It comes without warning

this image—the delicate foot and thigh
all sexual and full of fine meaning,

the liquid eye, shrewd and sorry.
For a moment we are sisters

Gretel and Gretel
lost in the dark and other wildlife

breathing, breathing.

Spite—Homage to Sylvia Plath

I stamped my feet and shook my fist and wept,
I wanted to be one of that glamorous sorority of the dead,
to feel the rib cage opened, the knocking of the heart let out,
I wanted to lie with the paperweight of the Bible on my chest;
I wanted the return, the rebirth, to be the root you fell over,
the curb of earth that made you stumble. I wanted to be the little
poisonous selves that grew up in your gardens, the henbane,
and belladonna, the lovely, misnamed hens-and-chickens;
I wanted revenge, to be the meek inheriting, beyond hurt and worry,
I wanted to come back as the vegetal, the spectacular amphibian welter
of the swamp, the pond, the marsh, the fen, to begin again and again,
I wanted to be no mind, all flesh, no thinking, all feeling, just *IS*
taking everything into its bog, its tar pit, into the locked box of unbeing.

Big Black Car

> . . . anything with wheels
> is a hearse in the making.
> Richard Miller

I thought, You'll never get me
anywhere near that motor's flattened
skull, the hoses' damp guts, the oil
pan with its tubes and fluids; I thought,
I'll never ride the black bargello
of the treads or be locked up
behind its locks and keys,
or stare at the empty sockets
of those headlights, the chrome
grill so glazed with light it blurs—
oily, edible, about to melt.
You'll never get me into that back seat,
the ruptured upholstery hemorrhaging
batting is not for me, nor the spooky
odometer, nor the gas-gauge letters
spilled behind the cracked,
milky glass. The horn, like Saturn,
is suspended in its ring of steering wheel;
and below it the black tongue of the gas pedal,
the bulge of the brake, the stalk
of the stick shift, and I thought, You'll never . . .
But here I am, and there in the window
the tight black street comes unzipped
and opens to the snowy underthings,
the little white stitches and thorns
of a starry sky, and there, beyond
the world's open gate, eternity
hits me like a heart attack.

The Out-of-Body Experience,

the extraterrestrial view,
   as though to die
      were to fly around
in the airplane
   of the mind
looking down on
   (from a great distance,
dwarfed and vivid)
   the Amazonian
wandering of the guts
      exposed,
looking at that me that is
      unkempt and wild, a trickle
from the tidal pool,
      wandering, wavering, and free.

Not to close things, but to open them,
   is the line drawn
      ruthlessly
the way mother drew
      her open sewing scissor
over the swollen belly
   of the melon.

So this is the way out,
   the sweet dishevelment, the delight
      of disorder,
to let go, and suddenly,
      we are in the cemetery,
dressed in the strict black dress
      the paperweight
of the Bible on my chest.

All the willows weeping,
     are not symbols for me
         but symbols for me
they stand, staunchly
     rooted in the black
rainy margin of this
     aerial photograph:
I am the river
     going over the spillway
like oiled bath water,
     a colder cold, a dark
dark.

What Dying Was Like

First I lay down
and then my senses began their climb
into the dark above me. Seeing, hearing
leapt away like goats I saw once in that hill
town in Tuscany, or like the day I stood and looked
on the Mediterranean's voluptuous and wrinkled bed,
now I gazed down on the immense miniature of this
landscape: the chimney of the throat stove in,
the collar of the larynx undone, even the knotted
grain of thumbprint was worn away. Good-bye thumb,
and wrist, licked back by all the tiny hungers of ants
to the bare tree shape of bare bone.
Winter had come and I was lunch, sumptuous, I who had been
a thin weed, a hank, was now a wide meadow, a marsh,
slick, fetid, damp, a swamp, I brewed and stank
until, mercifully, we came to the brain's convolvulus,
that wet coral, oceany and spacious, even that must be
lugged away like a big vegetable; I was an orphan,
and looked down now on the prairie, the waving
grass that licked up the last that I'd become,
but *I* looked down on them, there was that *I,*
a terrible cloud, a thinking wind.
That was the final terror, that I wept and could not leave the flesh.

What Did You Expect?

The Heavenly Father to damn and bless,
to dole out, in the parlor of the Everlasting,
his kicks and kisses, to say, Come here
my wretched brat, my darling?

Or that you would be enclosed
in swaddling of the crypt
like a ring in a jewelry chest?
You will not be saved up,

you will be exhausted, spent,
in the raptures of the gnats.
The great debauch of possibility
is just beginning; you will be

unlimited, a multitude as pale
as the ears of the fungus listening
to the earth go soft. You will never
want to go back to being locked up

in that little black closet of living.

The Poet in Heaven

Here in Heaven's small hotel
I have arranged my little life,
a place to eat at midday,
a place to have a drink at night.

Dying was a breathless ride,
the billboards flying past,
and then in that dark car's
dark window, like Texaco,

bloomed Heaven's swank.
And now the moon is rising
on all my lost remembrance:
I was a sheaf of wheat

unbound, or the grass razed,
or the shadows' shuddering
run before the scythe;
that was what it was to die.

And now I am the clouds:
a storm in small white dresses,
a ghostly rout that kneels
above the cut field's eye.

Three weeks and I've become
one who wind rumples and pets,
one who crawls across the sky
to watch her shadow in the dust.

What Heaven Is

What is Heaven, after all, but Chaos
neatened up into the Good, the Bad,
the Undecided, those rakes and corseted
mamas who wait in the foyer for the cool
unguent of the Beyond, their fortune

of Tomorrows, while my Soul
has come to be courted, wooed,
to be won over to the Good. Or not.
After all, while the industrious
set their grindstones to their noses,

their wheels to their shoulders,
I have been a great exuberant
fund of misbehavior. Like the sea—
that indolent lagoon lapping at the sand
and creeping toward the barbecue—

I teach by showing what not to do.
Like the lily, I neither toil nor spin
but simply am—appareled in beauty,
unworthy, unearning, unProtestant
and slightly screwy, really, because

who in her right mind would not want
the Prince of Love? So blonde? So tall?
So good? In the great body of great
works, I am an inexplicability;
like Penelope, I can't decide, I am

that tousled, sweating heroine
at the blackboard, head bowed,
whose sponge erases, like damp

prose, the right and wrong in one
bold stroke and leaves only

that blurred and blurry path between
this lesson and the next, what she
was supposed to know and didn't.
I am a pebble under the boot
of history, a loose thread,

nothing, really, the unimportant
and, therefore, immortal.

Homage to Dickinson

I've never longed for the annulments of Heaven,
nor for Hell, that orgy of repenting,
but have wanted the loneliness of this
slender room and bed, the cool neatness
of being dead: to be reduced, cleaned out,
a manageable mess, nothing left but knobs
and buttons, the skull an empty crock,
the pelvis a washed plate, the ribs laid
tidily, side by side. And I would be gone,
not that stern black dress, not that thing
with the Bible on her breasts. I would be
nothing but one narrow room of sepulcher,
one barred window where traffic never brings
its soot, the ear clean and empty as a scrubbed cup,
the tongue at rest and I, free at last, the window
of myself cast open, and all the sweet lament
of mourners throbbing in the distance, the angels'
white blouses pinned to the line of the horizon.
I would be alone, alone, in my maidenly
tomb, my own woman. Finally. And forever.

The Dig

Beyond the dark souks of the old city, beyond the Dome of the Rock
gray and humped and haunted, beyond the eyes of the men at the café
where they drink their thimblefuls of hot tea, beyond the valley
with its scar of naked pipe, the perfect geometrical arcs of irrigation,
and someone incising a dark furrow in a field, some plowman's black
gutter opening through the green, she is waist deep in this open grave,
staring at the delicate puzzle of my feet. Beyond her, in the shadow
of Tel Hesi, daubing and dampening the earth, another woman finds
the faint brickwork of floor spidering the dust, on the hearth's
wedge-shaped arc of shadow a scattering of charred millet.
Nothing else for miles. Nothing but this bluff of ruin,
one decapitated tower, one "window" staved into the brick,
the bougainvillea crawling across a wall dragging its little bloody rags.
She is standing here thinking she cannot bear the way this foot—
my foot—wants to step out of the earth. I don't care. I am using her
to leave the grave. And so we go on. We go on until we cannot go on
deepening my grave, and the trowel hits stone and I lie staring
while she makes the earth recede, reaches in and pulls me out,
my jaw wired shut by roots, my skull so full of dirt that suddenly
the intricate sutures come loose and, in her hands, the whole head opens.
In the shallow setting where I lay is the small triangular sail
of a scapula, the ribs like the grill of a car. She bones me like a fish.
She lays the little pieces, the puzzling odds and ends, into the dishes
of shellac and formalin. Wearily, I lean my reassembled head,
sutures rich with glue, against the wall of the filled beaker.
A fine sweat of bubbles on my chin. All night, through the window
of my jar, I watch her mend with glue and wire the shallow
saucer of my pelvis. We are nothing. Earth staring at earth.

Coda (in the Form of Notes)

The Beginning

"The Planet Krypton": At night, if the wand of the Geiger counter is held into the wind on the motel's roof, you can hear the spit and hiss of fallout. It is the voice of radium released from the earth. What must that be like, after centuries sealed in the marrow? The giddy stretch, the sinuous unlocking, the lift and catapult out of matter into the huge, wobbly, weightless tonnage of the explosion. The detonation has always sounded like a sob of relief. I can see it from here. It looks like a baby's rattle, the glittering, luminous bulb of the blast.

And now you see me. I am sitting, typing by the window, a thin woman in a flowered housedress. Perhaps you wonder who I am. I am the voice-over. I am the writer. My hand is on the rattle of the bomb. And this is my story. I was poor. I wrote. I killed myself.

"The Night Man at the Blue Lite": Outside my window the neon, glazed with rain, drips like an earring. The neon at the Blue Lite is amazingly, unsettlingly, sinisterly elaborate. But inside, the rooms are pure Nevada. The linoleum is so glazed with wax it seems watery and transparent. The sink is dusted with a light talcum from the Bon Ami. An iron bed, a deal dresser, those chunks of glass for pulls, beveled and screwed into the drawer front with a chrome screw. You could unscrew them and use them for ear bobs. They are little lamps and eyes, friends, protectors. They are the room's only jewelry, and they look delicious, cool, slick, and glossy, as though you could put them in your mouth.

"For Me at Sunday Sermons, the Serpent": Ely in its littleness is almost Oriental; it is where I found, to quote Bachelard's description of Hieronymus Bosch, "immensity in the miniature." The arbors and shadowed glades and roses of the oilcloth on the table were where I first learned to see in the Chinese manner, "every accidental

70

crack or dent." When I learned Chinese, I found it made from the "shish" sound all these words: history, city, lion, ten, corpse, stone, and teacher, and I thought of the story of stone soup, of trickery and scarcity, of turning something not much into something. This suits the housewife in me. I trimmed, from the ragged silken length of a dead rattler I saw once on the road to Ely, the serpent in the garden, the scarlet cummerbund.

Beginning Again

I have never told anyone this: When we first moved to Ely, my mother and I lived in a residential hotel. I don't remember the name of it, or the exact street. When I look back on it, it rises up out of the landscape like those mysterious mountains in George Herriman. But this pile of moldering stone, dark, singular, piercing, is driven like a stake into my heart. My mother was working, and I was perpetually ill with influenza. It was during this time my heart developed its stutter, its limp, those pendulous and weighty moments when the next beat seemed to drip from it achingly, infinitely slowly, and never arrive, like Dali's clocks.

Past and Present

How unlikely that a woman of my background, I who was most *American* (taking that word at its lowest common denominator: small town, western, granddaughter of hicks and pioneers), would find herself abroad. How could I fund it? The ways were unsavory. In fact, I was for a time living in Trastevere, modeling for a fairly well known Roman artist. Because the only way I had of making money was as a model, I spent a terrible amount of time worrying about my appearance. I was at the mercy of seamstresses and laundresses the way some men are at the mercy of loan sharks and bookies. Many of these poems were composed during that period. Incidentally, the only photograph of me is from the same period. It was taken in my studio. A glass door opens onto a small garden, green and seedy; there is a little lavatory and several huge windows that show the Tiber, where ships float by. I am wearing a rose and a Spanish shawl.

"Bella Roma": My poetry, as you can see, has been repeatedly diminished and deformed by the actual. Every moment of transcendence plummets to an anxious consideration of the economic terms of my life: food, shelter, and so on. So, too, do all these poems hint at a thematic concern I've dealt with more directly elsewhere: I have been highly involved in "the romance of not being listened to." This accounts for the sense of the soliloquist in much of my work. At times, I may have achieved a peculiar originality because one premise of my writing is this: I have had total liberty because I have had total anonymity. As I wrote in a letter to a friend, "All my life it has been as though I am already dead."

"On Waking after Dreaming of Raoul": In Ely I was the established figure of a single woman—the one in charge of maidenly jobs—a librarian, a waitress. I was, however, no maiden. Indeed, I indulged in a show of libido that seems almost avant-garde in a town like that. I had more than one romantic connection, including a "Mr. Rumens," the owner of the dry goods store, who "left his galoshes beneath my bed" (my euphemism) and "grimaced at climax."

The Hereafter and After That

"Far": Far away from here a train is threading down the tracks, tugging its trail of noise and light. The tracks are a scar, a leveled stair. Here, there is no up, no down, only near and far and farther. The sun leaks across the horizon at dawn and is sponged up at dusk by distance. That is our most lavish resource, invisible yet actual. Everything is planed down by distance, this turbulence of distance, this bulge and swell and ebb of pure distance, unpolluted and plenteous, unmined, primitive.

"The Dig": This poem makes me think of the Michelangelos of the Sistine Chapel. I cannot guess at the reasons for Michelangelo's blasphemy, but standing before the "Last Judgment," one suddenly realizes that the most horrified and horrifying figures in the fresco are those of the resurrected. They are being hauled up from their depths back into flesh, dragged up, kicking and screaming, out of the dark anonymous background, by their heels and the scruffs of their necks, in a kind of Christian instant replay. Their arms reach out to the dark that is the grave, lost to them. And there is one figure who, through a trick of illusion, twisted halfway toward the viewer, one foot upraised so that we see him from below, his foot flexed in a walk in midair, his sole exposed, as though his next step can only fall on the surface that is the very air of the chapel in which the viewer stands, seems about to walk out into his life. Isn't this what resurrection would be: to be alive in the now, to exist now, this moment, even as I write this. And the look on that face, the look of horror and disgust and terror. I would expect such looks from the damned; but from the saved?

HOTEL FIESTA

Black Sedans, Long Limousines

Let dust remember, let dung remember
at the gate . .

Frying Trout while Drunk

Mother is drinking to forget a man
Who could fill the woods with invitations:
Come with me he whispered and she went
In his Nash Rambler, its dash
Where her knees turned green
In the radium dials of the '50s.
When I drink it is always 1953,
Bacon wilting in the pan on Cook Street
And mother, wrist deep in red water,
Laying a trail from the sink
To a glass of gin and back.
She is a beautiful, unlucky woman
In love with a man of lechery so solid
You could build a table on it
And when you did the blues would come to visit.
I remember all of us awkwardly at dinner,
The dark slung across the porch,
And then mother's dress falling to the floor,
Buttons ticking like seeds spit on a plate.
When I drink I am too much like her—
The knife in one hand and in the other
The trout with a belly white as my wrist.
I have loved you all my life
She told him and it was true
In the same way that all her life
She drank, dedicated to the act itself,
She stood at this stove
And with the care of the very drunk
Handed him the plate.

The Sleeping

I have imagined all this:
In 1940 my parents were in love
And living in the loft on West 10th
Above Mark Rothko who painted cabbage roses
On their bedroom walls the night they got married.

I can guess why he did it.
My mother's hair was the color of yellow apples
And she wore a velvet hat with her pajamas.

I was not born yet. I was remote as starlight.
It is hard for me to imagine that
My parents made love in a roomful of roses
And I wasn't there.

But now I am. My mother is blushing.
This is the wonderful thing about art.
It can bring back the dead. It can wake the sleeping
As it might have late that night
When my father and mother made love above Rothko
Who lay in the dark thinking *Roses, Roses, Roses.*

Of Your Father's Indiscretions
and the Train to California

One summer he stole the jade buttons
Sewn like peas down Aunt Ora's dress
And you, who loved that trail of noise and darkness
Hauling itself across the horizon,
Moths spiraling in the big lamps,
Loved the oily couplings and the women's round hats
Haunting all the windows
And the way he held you on his knee like a ventriloquist
Discussing the lush push of grass against the tree's roots
Or a certain crookedness in the trunk.
Now everything is clearer.
Now when the train pulls away from the station
And the landscape begins to come around, distant and yet familiar,
That odd crease of yellow light
Or the woods' vague sweep framed in the window forever
Remind you of the year you were locked up at the Hotel Fiesta
While father went out with fast black minks.
And how wonderful it was
When he was narrow as a hat pin in this tux
And to have come all that way on his good looks.
How wonderful to have discovered lust
And know that one day you would be on its agenda
Like the woman who drank and walked naked through the house
In her black hat, the one you used to watch
Through a stammer in the drapes.
In that small town of cold hotels, you were the girl in the dress,
Red as a house burning down.

The Dig

He is filling the bucket with stones
And bringing the darkness up on a braided rope.
This will go on all day between the elm and iron gate.
The galvanized tin sings when it touches the rough balk
And the winch listens and the rope grows warm.
All day he has raised the dirt into this heaven of air.
I did not help. I poked my cup into the round
Eye of the bucket. I watched the shadows
Crawl inside and the wind limp stiffly
Through the little crooked places of tree and brandy.
All day he brings the darkness up until my heart
Is the bucket's round O of perpetual astonishment.
I put my hand across my eyes and listen
To the winch wind the rope around its shaft
And when I look a lizard is putting
Into my husband's hand her white
Stomach where one blue vein rides
From the groin to the throat.
I could have watched forever that slow work of muscle
In her neck, and something in the way he held her
Made me think of what we saw in ancient Eglon once:
A woman buried with her head in her lap, the cure
For infidelity, the old lust over-ended by the axe.
My husband worked all one night and in the end
I think he grew to love her, especially there,
With the earth on her like a black wing.

I Dream I Love You under the Pine, under the Poplar

I lie down
Always the same way

As though struck, anyway, I lie down
Again and again

Because I am young
And you are stroking me

Resinous branch, slowly, slowly,
A horse arises from that distant

Luxury of poplar—
Like silver breathed on—

The whole tree turns a bright
Haze in the wind.

It's you again, lacewing.
I live behind my eyes

At the eave and gable of myself
Thick with the larks

And the bells from whose lead throats
Cries topple, the unattainable

Brought close. From here I can see
Lilies and underneath the bulb

Like a sick extremity
Swollen, inert,

A vine vagrant along a limb.
I have read that on a bridge

In Nagasaki you can see
The shadow of a man still mounting

The shadow of a horse.

Berlin Interior with Jews, 1939

This is the year Europe looks up in sublime disregard
From the margin between two wars' classic accessories.
I am tired of the standard pictures of the Jews.
Even the Black Forest reminds me of my grandfather
Whose watch hands were tiny as pine needles.
I am tired of the fire twisting on the hearth where the maid
Brews hot mint tea in the middle of summer,
Tired of the sweet lip of the glass she lifts
To her mouth, tired of the reading of the *Aeneid*
And Dido lying down on the burning pyre—
Good-bye, good-bye the fire whispers to her flesh
Although no one listens. I am tired of my grandmother
Having to stand at the window to watch a train
The trickle of darkness at the horizon, slow, slightly crooked.
This is the year only the lamplight sleeps
Against her breast, the year she will wear her husband's
Gloves to bed because the buttons at the wrist,
Small, shiny as the eyes of her parakeet,
Stare as though they know her and this is the year
The maid in her red shawl bending to the kettle
On the hearth resembles a flame blown down by wind
And is about to be snuffed back to the wick of her black shoes.

When Father Decided
He Did Not Love Her Anymore

Tonight I will remember the model
With the wide, sad mouth
Who used to pose for father
Because I love the dangers of memory,
The boarded window and door,
Rooms where one bare bulb
Makes shadows swell up the wall.
And yet I recall only vaguely
The way her hem rustled on the floor
Like sand against tin
Laisse-moi tranquille, epicier,
It is said because I want it to
Say something memorable.
I want her back
That brilliant, farfetched woman
Who drank coffee in our garden
And the days father fed me
Absinthe through a sugar cube
So I would be asleep by noon
And wake to find Ramona posing
Naked with a tambourine.
Tonight the whole world is a garden
In which the immortal whispers
Something about art
And its opportunities:
Memory like a bolt of silk
In a tailor's arms
Can be made into anything
Especially misfortune,
Especially the year Ramona spent
In a wrath almost biblical

And so far from the world
Not even the moon could find
Her study in Paris
Where the doors opened to the river.

Grandmother Zoltana, Tunisia,
Early '50s—Two Photographs—Before
Her Death and at the Funeral

Even now it makes me thirsty to see her leaning in the doorway
Peeling peaches with her teeth.
Behind her rises the geometry of mosques and houses,
The ceaseless wheedling of a fountain—
These are the year of my voluptuous youth
And how cool it is when she washes
The soft stumble of broken stones leading to our house.
Somewhere inside I am watching the sweep of her hem
As she comes up from the beach and sits drinking beer
From a wet brown bottle and tells me good-bye
And good-bye whisper the cisterns of sweet water
Hidden under Carthage, good-bye the oars of the quinqueremes,
The harbor, and the way the fire whispers in her ears
As she stews four red peppers with wine and oil.
—This is the summer I grow afraid of the dark
Transforming itself into long sedans
Like those in the left-hand corner of the second photograph
Where boys are writing Arabic in the dusty windshields
And grandmother lies, attended by her priest.
In a long closet a man's silk tie lisps in my ear.
That night I undress in the gloom with grandfather watching
My hands nibble at their buttons and then
I am there: each nipple a boutonniere
Like the ones worn by men with thin black hair who carry
Grandmother and then me to bed.

Ordinary Objects

Hic et ubique?
　　　　Hamlet to the ghost

I am letting them stand
For everything I love:

The light's unsteady scale
Across the glass, the hard

Brown grit of ants among the roses,
The bittersweet—

Everywhere I look I will see
Italy. The flowers will be full

Of prisons and churches,
Of women in black dresses, full

Of motorcycles and genuflecting.
The nightshade's dark, crooked stem

Is your street
And the water in the vase the sea's

Horizon tilting with the tilt
Of your ship. I am going to let

The daffodil be your mistress.
She is tired of you and stands

Looking at her feet.
In the fan's slow wind

The curtains reach for you.
I am full of grief. I am going

To lie down and die and be reborn
To come back as these roses

And wind myself thorn by
Thorn around your house

To fit into the nutshell
And the flat seed, the scar,

The door, the road, the web,
the moon's bald envious eye

Staring at you through the drapes.

Dream about the Old Mosaic
Found in a Syrian Orchard

I have come through
The sudden starlight of gunfire

To view on another fragment
Of tessellated floor

Another Dido.
Over the beehive ovens' imbricate roofs

Smoke is gathering, over the boy
Teasing hoops down tilted streets,

Over nighties in the wind.
They seem to want to come—

Through all the long luxury of shade
Between rug merchant and public bath—

Into the orchard with its blur of plums.
This is heaven, so cold my teeth ache,

Even midsummer when the sun is the color
Of shaved pine beneath a pot.

A woman is lying oddly marred on a pyre.
All that is left of the rest of the world is a hand.

In the dream I am a green hill with an eye.
Nothing, really, earth staring at fire.

The Photograph of My Father
at an Early Exhibit of Arshile Gorky

Here he is standing beside Agony—sad and proprietary—
While women in silk stockings whisper as they pass, mistaking him
   for Gorky.
They think he is there to admire himself, but I know
He is waiting for me, hands in his pockets because of the dirt under
   his nails. Beside him a lover smokes like a gun.
Suppose I were she and after this photograph was taken
We had gone out joyriding in the black sedans of the 1940s
Past the hotel where Grandmother's teeth smiled at us from a glass
   of water,
Past the back porch of the Cook Street house in Denver
Where he used to wear his red kimono with Mt. Fuji rising from the
   mist,
Past Paris, past red Datsuns whizzing past Rue Baudelaire
And rooms filled with the chug chug of love, past all shores
Where the sea pours its cool threats and past and past
And past until the darkness carried us into the forest
Like two stones in its pocket—blind and still and immortal
As anything on earth.

The Photograph of Ramona Posing while Father Sketches Her in Charcoal

Father is transforming Ramona
Into a streamline of flesh
Smudging the nipple with his thumb
In the tough, awkward way
Children rub their eyes when tired.
The sea is smooth as oiled stone again
Between Cagnes-sur-Mer and Cap Bénat
And the shadows full of models' empty shoes
Because this is 1938 and the tedium and heat
Of the Côte d'Azur.
Even Ramona is boring in the slick
Cool silver of her flesh.
Life is not pretty
Although she does not believe it.
This girl whose gold tooth
Polished with his tongue
Could make anyone forget the wild buttocks of Rubens
And fill the fields with weeping painters
For whom the world has become a studio
Of beautiful forgeries.
Life is not pretty
Although they do not know it yet—
And in that heat
And the streets full of Germans.

Apology

Tonight I lie staring into the unlit neighborhood
And remembering Maria Bauder at whose windows
I threw stones from behind a trellis of dead roses.
She was German and that year school resurrected
The war in Europe until all night long trains
Of dead children flashed past like light
On a hypnotist's gold watch. It has been a long time
Since that evening when, full of sulk and swagger,
I leaned in my mother's dormer watching as Maria entered
From her bare yard to ours filled with the soft
Exaltations of light. From the branches of black
Walnut the great weight of the moon leaned out.
I overheard her accusations and then came down
Into the issuance of my name and stood on the porch
In the chilly updraft of self-pity and said I was sorry
Under a sky tall and decorated with stars as a general.

Self-Portrait

Tiresome, tiresome is the poet
Recumbent on the davenport
Lost in raptures of self-regard.
Give me poetry but pure
Before *charcuterie* and *bistro*
And distracted poses in tilted mirrors.
I am what is wrong with America.
Standing debauched, bereft,
Empty-handed for first one
Eternal verity and then another,
I am tired of all my yawn and barter.
How boring beauty is:
All chives and savannas,
The lush populations of grasses,
Are one vast atelier for the abstract.
Despite my lovely diction
I am going to die
Lying on an iron bed in stocking feet.
Oh no, oh no says the portrait
But so beautifully it is almost yes.

The Artists

... darkness is awake upon the dark.
                                    D. H. Lawrence

I was not alive when you posed in silk trunks for Matisse
Or kissed Ruth Roman in front of the theater.
But I remember Mikonos:
The day we amazed ourselves, undressed, and walked
From noon into the wide syllables of water.
I saw your long eyes close.
I am in this picture:
White, masked, falling, here
Where everything is falling
As the clouds change their minds overhead.
It was warm, then cold—we fought the warnings and forgot
Everything except that conspiracy
Taking us league after untranslated league
Until gravity relinquished us.
And then the darkness settled, we had arrived
At the place where ships went down;
You hovered before me casting a long light onto the wreckage.
Father, something happened here: the craft had been rapturous
On water and the helmsmen, dozing, thinking their job done,
Woke to find dolphins in the masts.
I imagine these voyagers finally gave up,
Opened their lips,
And went as simply as you
Or I into that visitation.

Patient

I remember my mother on her hard knees
Complaining to the floor about the rich,
Her voice rough across the slick rise
Of their culpabilities, her hand moving
From the zinc bucket to the floor
Beside the bed in which I waited, sick,
For the cold kiss of salt and wet bread.
She fed me that lump on a tarnished spoon
While long limousines climbed the tipped hill
To the house where the man my mother loved
Shared the bright, empty plate of his table
With his wife. At night my mother would lie
Small and white as an egg in an apron, silent
As a snake laying its green throat on a pillow
Of stone. She thought about him until his face,
Like a moth wing worn away by the soft
Fascination of a child, crumbled to odds and ends
Under the tall black chill of common sense.

Of My Father before the War

Suppose I were leaning in a doorway in Marseilles watching a volley
Of far clouds while two men quilted the water with their nets.
Suppose I were the one caught by the rain while the sea rinsed the docks
And gave the pilings a fat and oily slap
And suppose everywhere the cruise ships were setting off,
Violins swooning in the ballrooms, each liner lit up
Like Versailles. *Après moi le déluge,* I might say
As the great fleets of 1938 left me with the smoke
From my cigarette unraveling in my mustache.
And suppose one ship with a huge feather of steam above the stack
Let down its gangplank and I watched a woman in a veiled hat
Come hurrying forward. Father, this blur in the tripped shutter
Might be someone who could smuggle you out.
But what if I were grouped with all the houses in the cool
Silver of February and one garret were filled with the work
Of my blunt brushes. What if I had keys hidden in my pocket
And a lover lazily unzipping her dress when the woman who could save me
Waved and cried and disembarked into the vast nonchalance of France.

MISS CHRISTINA, MISS LORRAINE

Let the wild beasts and the sky's birds eat
  and remember.
Let all of them remember, so I can rest.
                              Yehuda Amichai

After Your Letter of Elegant Good-bye

This is a road where I could die for love
Nosing the car toward the black falls

The noise of an axe working
Its own way through woods that stand between me

And a view so suicidally inviting
A man has decided to build a house.

This is where I kill the lights,
Coast out toward the cutting of two-by-fours.

Beyond the skeletal bedroom, nothing but down:
The forest is fine and dry as loose handfuls

Pulled from a hen.
Even in this heat he has built a fire,

The mouth of a barrel crammed with burning lath
A blossom of sour smoke growing from charred strata.

I envy him the pines that lavish
His roof with soft touches, the bell of millet

He tied on a low branch swings silently
Above a town tipped with steeples.

I am so tired I could lie down among these trees
Until I was nothing

And let the earth take one slow liberty
After another.

You Tell Me

You tell me you're the stranger in bad weather,
I'm the girl hitching east in your dream.
You tell me I think it's beautiful:
The storm approaching on the solid body of wheat,
Clouds knotting the light
And each root connecting in the furrows
Until the acres tear under the thresher
As easily as old silk.
Which is not your freedom.
You have chosen to see how the sun is blank as a tack,
And we come past Leadville lonely, fighting,
On roads where people die each winter
Parked like lovers in their cars.
You try to explain about the workers,
Barges, coal, pipe, some small town
Where the dead have their churches and we stop
To watch a seizure of light in an open door.
I am slightly drunk, a young widow
With a tiny gun, riding out of Wichita
Toward Pittsburgh—all those broken homes,
The smell of sulphur and the fire
Where men exhaust themselves in shifts,
You tell me.

Desire

This is not Turner's Venice,
Not all the light is let loose across the canals,
The low clefts of little waves.
This is Pittsburgh where the air is sulphurous
And the water landlocked, slowed by waste and those small
    iron bridges.
But even here we have discovered desire, like Columbus
Who was looking for the end of the world and stumbled on
    continents.

In the elms there are supple constellations of light.
We are sitting in the yard and I, too, am hoping for the end
Of something, of the world, maybe,
That great still perfect lip and those little boats going off.

But it is August and this
The most familiar place in the world,
Calm water, boats, channels
And beautiful, too, those little bridges
Leading back and forth across the river.
Here in our own backyard we can find
The rare acres of stars, the thin wind
Abating in the huge green hesitations of the trees.

Tourists

In Tunis we try to discuss divorce
And dying but give up to lounge

With rug merchants under a plum tree.
From its corner the lamb's severed head

Watches the flies drink from its eyes
And its fat disappear into the fire.

The light rinses the edge of your sandal,
The two wasps that ornament the blur

Of screened window. My grandmother
Would have loved a night like this.

In the wind chimes I can hear her tea cart
With its china rolling through Cook Street's

Stony yard one summer when I was always
Thirsty, and she moved like a figure

On a clock from lawn chair to the cart,
Or swabbed me with alcohol, or cut

My hair with the straight razor.
I was a week out of the hospital.

Beneath my breasts an incision was crossed
With stitches of surgical thread.

The scalpel came so close it gave
My heart a quick kiss. I nearly died.

Years later I can still see the skin
Flutter on the inside of my left breast

And my heart limps like a great uncle
Who, because he was a Jew and lame,

Was dragged by cossacks across the steppes.
He became a friend asking a favor

Of a horse who ran so hard, so perfectly
Hard, that the green grass rose to meet him.

She Is Six

She sleeps on a cot in the living room.
This is her father's mother's house.
And in the kitchen the men run their knife blades
Across the oilcloth with roses on the table
And Grandmother cooks them steak and eggs.
She is pretending to be asleep but she is listening
To the men talking about their friends
And Grandmother in her white dress
Walks back and forth past the door
And a hand reaches for salt and water.
Her father talks about divorce.
Now it is quiet.
Grandmother has left, her tight stockings
Showed rainbows,
And someone's upstairs undressing,
His dog tags making faint noise.
Her father walks into the room.
He is naked and there are certain
Parts of him that are shadows.
And he pulls the blankets to the floor
And then the sheet—as if not to wake her—
And he lifts her up and whispers his wife's name—
Rachel, Rachel
And he takes her hand, small with its clean nails,
And he puts it to the dark:
Oh Rae, oh Rachel he says
And over his shoulder she can see
The long hall mirror framed in black wood
And she smells lavender in her father's hair
And then he gets up, first onto his hands
And knees like someone playing horse,
And puts her on the chair
And she sits and rocks like a deaf woman.

Discovering the Photograph
of Lloyd, Earl, and Priscilla

These are the great discoveries of my middle age:
This roadhouse in Omaha where Uncle Lloyd is nursing
Highballs with an ex-G.I. named Earl.
She's here, too, leaving a damp pink parenthesis
On the rim of her glass. The men are bored
But the girl whose name hisses like an iron across damp shirts
Peels open a pack of cigarettes and fills the room with smoke.
I have always wanted a coziness like theirs:
Rain touching the roof and someone trying to explain about Labor—
I might have been the waitress mopping up tips with a damp hand,
The one who loved Earl all those years while toting armloads
Of cobblers made from berries tiny as black caviar.
Tonight in an open window someone's stylus unzips a faint piano.
It must be 1947, Earl slicing salted melon from the rind,
Drinking the juice off his plate and the waitress going home
To count the dresser knobs until she falls asleep.
Tonight I find I envy the rain turning Omaha to daguerreotype,
Mud roads running amber as the veins in bad marble.
It is getting late. In the background beyond Earl and the waitress
There must be gardens. Roses, bowed down by their own heaviness,
Each day grow more perfect and more neighborly.
There must be graves and each separate grave is sending out
Its separate ghost.

Inventing Father in Las Vegas

If I could see nothing but the smoke
From the tip of his cigar, I would know everything
About the years before the war.
If his face were halved by shadow I would know
This was a street where an EATS sign trembled
And a Greek served coffee black as a dog's eye.
If I could see nothing but his wrist I would know
About the slot machine and I could reconstruct
The weak chin and ruin of his youth, the summer
My father was a gypsy with oiled hair sleeping
In a Murphy bed and practicing clairvoyance.
I could fill his vast Packard with showgirls
And keep him forever among the difficult buttons
Of the bodice, among the rustlings of their names,
Miss Christina, Miss Lorraine.
I could put his money in my pocket
And wearing memory's black fedora
With the condoms hidden in the hatband
The damp cigar between my teeth,
I could become the young man who always got sentimental
About London especially in Las Vegas with its single bridge—
So ridiculously tender—leaning across the river
To watch the starlight's soft explosions.
If I could trace the two veins that crossed
His temple, I would know what drove him
To this godforsaken place, I would keep him forever
Remote from war—like the come-hither tip of his lit cigar
Or the harvest moon, that gold planet, remote and pure American.

Elegy Written in the Vowels of Her Name

I have always loved Rogier Van Der Weyden's *Portrait of a Woman*
Because there is, between the little landscape of the hands—

Worldly like my grandmother's—and the impossible piety
In that face, a hidden commerce. It reminds me of the summer

My grandmother, brokenhearted, sat measuring a cool lapful
Of dried beans into a basin at her feet and how heavy

And gold as coiled rope those afternoons when the shadow
Of the pine came for its slow visits, dripping its dark

Shawls across her heart until I thought she would disappear.
Her body, stunned by stroke, dragged like a boat at anchor

Between the smell of scorched linen and the window,
Through which she could see yachts open the huge

Curve of reflected sky and sail away, bay by blue unvoyaged bay.

Enormous Leisure

I remember how you entered the water
Where the current murmurs to itself
Interrupted, now and then, by a flank of rock.
We lived in the mewsy streets around the theater
With names like "Hamlet," "Ophélie";
"Rue de l'Arbre Sec" led us out
Past the stiff gestures of shore pine
To the water and we would dip our oars and drift
Further to see the blunt-nosed pitch of the yacht
And the air was haunted with the smell
Of oiled steel and teak.

We were enamored of the dark,
The chipped green-blue of water,
Our vision jumbled as we pulled out,
Black masked, perched on the bow like two monkeys
And tumbled through the kelp whose fine hands
Parted to nothing
—The sudden huge blue pressure of the Atlantic
And your body, thick, whitish-green
Like shark or rare marble.
As we knew it would, the reef exploded
The fish running against us, the long leaps
And twists of kelp stoked by the current
And the absolute silence where we drifted and I saw you once—
Against the buckling window of the surface—
Scissoring your arms and legs
Like some distant felon running
From the enormous leisure of the light.

At the Magritte Exhibition

To a woman whose forehead is like a white veranda
You explain your apprenticeship with sorrow.
You and *Lola De Valence* are caught
Among museum goers, amid showers and the moths
Dragging their wet wings across the glass
To get a look at *La Vie Secrète*.
I imagine the damp reaches of Montauk
And the Hudson tarnished, cool and bitter
And beyond Manhattan, Malibu, surf lathering the rocks
Bad luck lying in her hammock, expectant.
I imagine you know America is laughing
And Belgium and France and you will go home
Brokenhearted to begin another canvas,
The roses, again, or Notre Dame. I believe
Magritte is shaking his head at your yellow taxi.
I believe the roses are wrong. All night
Their cool, insolent faces watch your house,
The roses putting their roots down onto the faces of the dead.

Looking for the Old Rosebud Cemetery

There is nowhere to go except this detour
And the motel whose lit name

Drips like a jeweled earring. In the lounge
A woman runs a bored finger along the keys

Of an upright and damps the pedal until the notes
Slow to one long blur of sound.

Nowhere to go, nothing for miles
Except this black coast

Of pine and the truckers hauling lumber up
And down the steep angulation of the divide

Or dozing on the washed out, raw shoulder
Of the highway, the radio tuned to a woman's

Low voice almost overcome by sorrow—
Two angels roam on that far shore.

Beautiful dead end. Where are you?
I stop to let things stand clear

In the headlights: a sparrow dipping its beak
Into a bright spatter of millet someone's thrown

And drive back blind to Denver.

What I Know about the End
of the Second World War

In L.A. someone is kissing Veronica Lake
And here, outside the window, the neon says *Hotel Clover.*
Trains haul copper all night through the quiet state
While Grandmother lays out knives in the parlor.
Down the long hall, guests slowly rock across each other,
Their skirts and trousers on the chairs.
It is raining. My mother comes into the room
And I can hear the slight noise of buttons and see
Her hands on her breasts, the way they follow
One another. And now she is all light, all shadow
Waltzing slowly in the room, hands on her forehead,
The sign outside repeating *Clover, Clover, Clover.*

On Returning to Carthage
to Excavate an Ancient Sacrificial Site

For the first time I could remember
Grandmother's hair breaking in a fine

Shiver from the braid,
Her house at the top of the sloped avenue

Below which the world grew small.
The Bay of Tunis stared—huge blue eye—

Until I was nothing, until I was not I
But someone who could wash out the urn burials

Of children sacrificed under every green tree
To Baal. How heavy, hot and bright the work

Of the boats whose nets gathered the sea
Into pleated wakes and then let go.

The water broke against the sloped stones
While I opened the round throats of those jars

And like my grandmother cleaning a pumpkin
Spooned out that mixture. All day I sent the tongue

Of hose water digging and found
There was no end to the possibilities of childhood.

It could be a splash of mud on the inner hollow
Of a curved jug, a group of gold beads.

Over and over the whole bone of the inner ear
Turned up intact like a bud of honey locust

About to blossom in my hands.
It could be anything. Even that.

Kiss

In the cooking pot my aunt's long spoon pets the lamb's
Severed head, anoints with oil its one terrible eye
Until it weeps at the flowers on her dress.
Where there was body once, now there is iron and fire.
I am here to help. I am here to put my hand under
The lamb's chin and tip it back as though for a kiss.
I am here to help the lamb with the axe
That halves the skull as I have heard my aunt halve
Her husband's name at night. *I/saac.*
The body cannot die. In the hard push of meadow
Behind the empty house I have seen the lamb's body
Ride a spit of peeled plum under my uncle's hand.
I have seen the lamb lie down in the fire and rise
To its cleft hooves. Through the dark doorway
Of the cut neck I have watched the heart leak
Fire and flower a dry foam of ash.
The body cannot die. I can see this.
When the throat is tilted to let the smoke loose
The lamb's shadow crawls forward, licks, then swallows
The whole rough tongue of stones where I lie.
It is too quiet. I can feel the uneven knocking
Of my heart like someone tired hobbling across a yard
To the plum tree that makes one shadow want to lie down
With another. I want to die. Death is nothing.
It is fire looking for a place to start. It is a word
On the tip of the lamb's halved tongue, a kiss strong enough
To carry the green wood into the meadow.

for Michael Harari

118

The Poet in the Garret in America

I come up here to be disembodied and abstract,
To feel the sycamore astir against my naked psyche.
All over the hill a swarm of windows lights up
As I sit watching the half-dead plum, one frail
Output of flower, one blossomy upfloat.
Mopery is my métier. I want to see something
Beyond this woman sleeping through the groan
Of airbrake and dead pine when truckers bear down
On Mount Sopris. By day she's a waitress
With a huge red hankie pinned above her heart;
By night she turns into poetry so magnificent
She leaves the whole world looking loutish
And obscure. America, I want to transcend you.
Like this cardinal in the sycamore I love
My own beautiful sensibility and have come here
To be issued an invitation as exact and stunning
As Eve's was in her green, frail, and sacramental
World. Under all my winsome diction, you and I
Are standing toe to toe, the diurnal, the divine.
America, I am still hopeful and a woman of my time.

Acknowledgments for *The Dig*

The author thanks the following publications in which these poems first appeared, sometimes in different versions and under different titles:

"The Technology of Love," "Rebirth," *American Poetry Review*
"Spite—Homage to Sylvia Plath," *Chronicle of Higher Education*
"Big Black Car," "Stone Soup," "What the Keyhole Was," *Georgia Review*
"The Poet in Heaven," *Hudson Review*
"The Planet Krypton," "Domestic Violence," *Kenyon Review*
"Dreaming of Rio at Sixteen," "Inspiration," *New England Review & Bread Loaf Quarterly*
"Seizure," "Drawing Rosie's Train Trip," "For Me at Sunday Sermons, the Serpent," "The Night Man at the Blue Lite," "Blonde Bombshell," "Riddle," "One Summer Hurricane Lynn Spawns Tornados as Far West as Ely," "This Is the Truth," *Ohio Review*
"The Dig," "The Past," "Outside Room Six," *Ploughshares*
"Whites," "A Red Kimono," "Chinoisserie," "What Ely Was," *Prairie Schooner*
"Heartsick," "On Waking after Dreaming of Raoul," *Southern Review*
"Inspiration, Two" "What Grieving Was," "Far," "Self-Portrait at Eighteen," *Three Rivers Journal*
"Homage to Dickinson," "What Did You Expect?" "What Heaven Is," "What Dying Was Like," *TriQuarterly*
"Inspiration" and "Blonde Bombshell" are anthologized in *New American Poets of the 90s,* ed. Jack Myers and Roger Weingarten (New York: David R. Godine, 1991). "For Me at Sunday Sermons, the Serpent" and "Inspiration" are in *An Ear to the Ground: An Anthology of American Poetry,* ed. Marie Harris and Kathleen Aguero (Athens: University of Georgia Press, 1989). In addition, "Inspiration" is in *The Anthology of Magazine Verse and Yearbook of American Poetry,* ed. Alan F. Rater (Beverly Hills, Calif.: Monitor, 1986–87) and in *Light Year '88,* ed. Bob Wallace (Cleveland: Case Western Reserve University, 1988).
A group of poems in this book was published as a chapbook, *The Technology of Love* (Omaha: Abattoir Editions, University of Nebraska, 1988).

Work on this book was generously supported by grants from the Commonwealth of Pennsylvania Council on the Arts.

I would also like to thank four people whose support and generosity were indispensable to the writing of this book: Maggie Anderson, Pat Dobler, Judy Vollmer, and Jeffrey Schwartz. *Ne plus ultra.*

Acknowledgments for *Hotel Fiesta*

The author and the publisher gratefully acknowledge the following publications where these poems first appeared:

"The Photograph of My Father at an Early Exhibit of Arshile Gorky," "The Last Two Photographs of My Father before the War," "Grandmother Zoltana, Tunisia, Early '50s—Two Photographs—Before Her Death and at the Funeral," "Of Your Father's Indiscretions and the Train to California," *American Poetry Review*

"The Sleeping," "She Is Six," *Extended Outlooks: The Iowa Review Collection of Contemporary Writing by Women*

"The Dig," "You Tell Me," *Georgia Review*

"Frying Trout while Drunk," "The Photograph of Ramona Posing while Father Decided He Did Not Love Her Anymore," *Poetry*

"What I Know about the End of the Second World War," "The Artists," *Prairie Schooner*

"Elegy Written in the Vowels of Her Name," "Patient," "Discovering the Photograph of Lloyd, Earl, and Priscilla," *Three Rivers Poetry Journal*

"Enormous Leisure," *Slow Loris Reader*

"Inventing Father in Las Vegas," *Virginia Center for the Creative Arts Anthology*

"Of Your Father's Indiscretions and the Train to California" (reprint), *Anthology of Magazine Verse and Yearbook of American Poetry, 1984*

"Berlin Interior with Jews, 1939," "Of Father's Indiscretions and the Train to California," "The Sleeping," "Frying Trout while Drunk," and "She Is Six" appear in the *Morrow Anthology of Younger American Poets* (New York: William Morrow, 1985).

I wish to thank The Virginia Center for the Creative Arts for a period of residence during which some of this book was written and the Pennsylvania Council on the Arts for a Creative Writing Fellowship.

Illinois Poetry Series

Laurence Lieberman, Editor

History Is Your Own Heartbeat
Michael S. Harper (1971)

The Foreclosure
Richard Emil Braun (1972)

The Scrawny Sonnets and Other
Narratives
Robert Bagg (1973)

The Creation Frame
Phyllis Thompson (1973)

To All Appearances: Poems New
and Selected
Josephine Miles (1974)

The Black Hawk Songs
Michael Borich (1975)

Nightmare Begins Responsibility
Michael S. Harper (1975)

The Wichita Poems
Michael Van Walleghen (1975)

Images of Kin: New and Selected
Poems
Michael S. Harper (1977)

Poems of the Two Worlds
Frederick Morgan (1977)

Cumberland Station
Dave Smith (1977)

Tracking
Virginia R. Terris (1977)

Riversongs
Michael Anania (1978)

On Earth as It Is
Dan Masterson (1978)

Coming to Terms
Josephine Miles (1979)

Death Mother and Other Poems
Frederick Morgan (1979)

Goshawk, Antelope
Dave Smith (1979)

Local Men
James Whitehead (1979)

Searching the Drowned Man
Sydney Lea (1980)

With Akhmatova at the Black
Gates
Stephen Berg (1981)

Dream Flights
Dave Smith (1981)

More Trouble with the Obvious
Michael Van Walleghen (1981)

The American Book of the Dead
Jim Barnes (1982)

The Floating Candles
Sydney Lea (1982)

Northbook
Frederick Morgan (1982)

Collected Poems, 1930–83
Josephine Miles (1983)

The River Painter
Emily Grosholz (1984)

Healing Song for the Inner Ear
Michael S. Harper (1984)

The Passion of the Right-Angled
Man
T. R. Hummer (1984)

Dear John, Dear Coltrane
Michael S. Harper (1985)

Poems from the Sangamon
John Knoepfle (1985)

In It
Stephen Berg (1986)

The Ghosts of Who We Were
Phyllis Thompson (1986)

Moon in a Mason Jar
Robert Wrigley (1986)

Lower-Class Heresy
T. R. Hummer (1987)

Poems: New and Selected
Frederick Morgan (1987)

Furnace Harbor: A Rhapsody of
the North Country
Philip D. Church (1988)

Bad Girl, with Hawk
Nance Van Winckel (1988)

Blue Tango
Michael Van Walleghen (1989)

Eden
Dennis Schmitz (1989)

Waiting for Poppa at the Smith-
town Diner
Peter Serchuk (1990)

Great Blue
Brendan Galvin (1990)

What My Father Believed
Robert Wrigley (1991)

Something Grazes Our Hair
S. J. Marks (1991)

Walking the Blind Dog
G. E. Murray (1992)

The Sawdust War
Jim Barnes (1992)

The God of Indeterminacy
Sandra McPherson (1993)

Off-Season at the Edge of the
World
Debora Greger (1994)

Counting the Black Angels
Len Roberts (1994)

National Poetry Series

Eroding Witness
Nathaniel Mackey (1985)
Selected by Michael Harper

Palladium
Alice Fulton (1986)
Selected by Mark Strand

Cities in Motion
Sylvia Moss (1987)
Selected by Derek Walcott

The Hand of God and a Few
Bright Flowers
William Olsen (1988)
Selected by David Wagoner

The Great Bird of Love
Paul Zimmer (1989)
Selected by William Stafford

Stubborn
Roland Flint (1990)
Selected by Dave Smith

The Surface
Laura Mullen (1991)
Selected by C. K. Williams

The Dig
Lynn Emanuel (1992)
Selected by Gerald Stern

My Alexandria
Mark Doty (1993)
Selected by Philip Levine

The High Road to Taos
Martin Edmunds (1994)
Selected by Donald Hall

Other Poetry Volumes

Local Men and *Domains*
James Whitehead (1987)

Her Soul beneath the Bone: Wom-
en's Poetry on Breast Cancer
Edited by Leatrice Lifshitz (1988)

Days from a Dream Almanac
Dennis Tedlock (1990)

Working Classics: Poems on In-
dustrial Life
*Edited by Peter Oresick and
Nicholas Coles* (1990)

Hummers, Knucklers, and Slow
Curves: Contemporary Baseball
Poems
Edited by Don Johnson (1991)

The Double Reckoning of Christo-
pher Columbus
Barbara Helfgott Hyett (1992)

Selected Poems
Jean Garrigue (1992)

New and Selected Poems, 1962–
92
Laurence Lieberman (1993)

The Dig and *Hotel Fiesta*
Lynn Emanuel (1994)